Caged Free Bird

Diary, Part 1

Hope

ARCHWAY
PUBLISHING

Archway Publishing books may be ordered through booksellers or by contacting:

Archway Publishing
1663 Liberty Drive
Bloomington, IN 47403
www.archwaypublishing.com
844-669-3957

ISBN: 978-1-6657-3266-6 (sc)
ISBN: 978-1-6657-3265-9 (e)

Library of Congress Control Number: 2022920009

Print information available on the last page.

Archway Publishing rev. date: 10/31/2022

Preface

"I have to remind myself that some birds aren't meant to be caged. Their feathers are just too bright. And when they fly away, the part of you that knows it was a sin to lock them up does rejoice. But still, the place you live in is that much more drab and empty that they're gone."

—*The Shawshank Redemption*

The year 2013 started off as good for me. I was interning at an amazing school as a student teacher. I was doing great at university. My friends and I had amazing relationships where we didn't have to be in contact 24/7; through the new world's technology, we still stayed close. And my love life was perfect. I was getting my bachelor's degree in teaching, and I loved being an intern. My students were wonderful. So was my life, I thought.

Then, May 11 became the unfortunate day when my

world abruptly stopped. I woke up with a camera in my face at 9:00 a.m., surrounded by cops with huge guns. I'm not exactly a gun enthusiast, so I'm not sure what those guns are really called, but I can testify that they were huge. I was at my boyfriend's house with his older sister. We were so close. I loved his family, sometimes more than I loved my own. Anyway, we got dragged to the police station, where it was clarified that we were in for drug dealing.

The night before, on a television news series I shall not name because of just how much I loathe it, a young man was caught in his car with a woman's purse overflowing with none other than bags of weed—oh, and a gram of cocaine—but I digress. This man was a "friend" of my boyfriend's at the time. He claimed the purse to be mine and the drugs to be my boyfriend's. Considering my boyfriend has a disability, I suppose the claim was credible. It was not the case, but credible. This explains the bombardment we experienced the next morning.

The hours of interrogation passed slowly on that lovely Saturday. My boyfriend, his sister, the man caught previously, several others, and I were caught up in the situation. Oh, the truths that came to light—they were shocking, and I was dumbfounded. I was, to say the least, blinded by love. As well, cops in Lebanon are idiots. Through my entries that follow, you will see to what extent, but until then, let's just settle on this Saturday afternoon. When the day was done, and all that could be said was said, we were informed that we would be put behind bars until the cops could figure that mess out.

Ever heard the term *blinded by love*? I did love my boyfriend, and because of his condition, I thought, *The medications must be what are making him so tired by the end of the night.* He slept a little more, and blamed it all on medication and pain. It was easy to believe. I was in love.

Keep in mind that we were told this would all take a couple of days since Sunday is the weekend and things don't really run up to speed here in Lebanon. A few days turned into eight months—eight months as an innocent accused drug dealer until they would figure out if I was innocent enough for bail before we even got to the final verdict. Welcome to Lebanon; the system takes so long to process you as a human being that you stop feeling like one eventually. And till today, the story has not ended. The story I'm writing here has just begun.

With a stolen pen and some papers, over the first twenty-two days in the small cell and my time moving jails throughout my eight months of imprisonment, a diary would randomly emerge from a wrongly imprisoned woman. In a country where "guilty until proven innocent" is a law abided by quite strictly, my story will be unraveled through my thoughts, my writings, and my afterthoughts from until a few months after I came out. The transformation is one I am proud of. In collecting my thoughts years later, I have taken parts of my diary from 2013 to sparingly today to portray, even in the slightest, the psychological and physical torment I went through. This experience, while the worst, is also the best, as I am now who I am because of it.

Chapter One

It was a dark day when I was thrown into that cell in Hbeish Police Station in Lebanon. I was with eleven other women, including the "friend" I was caught with that morning. That so-called friend left two days later, and I was alone. I was with eleven other foreigners from all over the world, including Kenya, Ethiopia, and several other countries around Africa. They were incredibly supportive and such beautiful women.

Days went by without using the bathroom or eating, and I barely drank any water. I smoked cigarette after cigarette, crying. Every day, the so-called detective's office would call me up to interrogate me in the harshest way possible. I was yelled at, screamed at, shown a gun to have me admit to something I didn't do, and I was threatened numerous times. They would do this to me several times a day for days on end, at all hours of the day, when I'd be least comfortable, including after midnight. They stripped me of my rights, I wasn't allowed to make any phone calls, I wasn't allowed my lawyer, and the worst part was that no one would come visit me. The only people who knew at this point were my aggrieved uncles. The detectives had me sign my interrogation papers knowing I did not read Arabic; I was only to find out days later I had signed confessions I did not make. I was desperate to get my voice out. I was desperate to get out.

The women in my cell left one by one, and a few days later, I found myself alone. It was a dark room, with the smallest window at the door for cops to pass by and check up on me every few hours. Some were good to me, and some were, of course, complete assholes. The cell was filthy, the walls were covered in offensive graffiti, and the "Arabic" bathroom in the corner heaved the most disgusting of smells all day. I had few pieces of clothing I could change into and showered probably three or four times in the twenty-two days I spent there. At some point, a gorgeous Ethiopian (whose name I'll keep to myself forever to hide her identity) would take care of me, making sure I ate at least once every two days. I still think of her every now and then, hoping she's okay.

For twenty-two days, I felt stuck in a moment. It was exhausting, and my body ached. I slept on the floor, as there were no mattresses. It was hard and cold. The ants crawling around me eventually became my friends when I fed them the various foods the officers would try to feed me. I didn't have a pillow, and I barely had my basic needs met. I read book after book to try to escape the harsh reality I was in. But it was impossible. It was incredibly impossible. I wrote so much my hand ached. I read what I wrote now and realized I wasn't stable in my head. I had so many thoughts, feelings, and fears pouring out of me that I suppose they just drove me mad. I was alone, and I was scared.

I was awoken with haste on the twenty-second day in the lonely little cell in Hbeish Police Station, up the street from my house, when someone called my name aloud. I realized it was still early morning and they must be calling to release me! I had never been so excited. I jumped up, forgetting the cold, hard floor and my cracking bones. I peeked my head out of the door's tiny window to see a cop come up to me and tell me to pack my things. I had the biggest smile plastered on my face. It quickly vanished when he said "because you're going to Baabda." The police officer had woken me up to tell me I was being transferred.

Baabda is a city that holds one of the harshest women's prisons in Lebanon. I was shocked. I felt like the wind had been knocked out of me. I quietly asked him to repeat what he had said, and when he did, I asked him to make sure. *That's impossible,* I remember thinking. Everyone had told me I would go home. Why would I go from a jail to a prison if this was about to end?

I was even more afraid. I was shaking and didn't know what to do. You see, "guilty until proven innocent" means you are treated as a convict even if you aren't. I was just a newbie. I was being transferred from jail to an official prison. Oh God, and now I knew it would be a long road before I could see the sun again.

Lebanon, Hbeish to Baabda
Prison, Sunday, June 2, 2013:

I packed my "things," which consisted of a few old undergarments and two or three dirty shirts. I removed my ripped pants, left them behind, and put on an old pair of sweatpants, only to realize I'd already lost so much weight in twenty-two days that they were slipping off me. Of course,

I left the room handcuffed and slowly walked upstairs with my head down to wait for the run-down van taking me on a two-hour trip; I would view through windows what I couldn't have. It was sickening.

I arrived at Baabda later that day, still shocked, my head hung low. The police officers there were mean, except for one or two, and I had never really liked women of this country to begin with. But now, to deal with Lebanese women who had power? It took everything I had to stay calm and not get angry. Instead, I tensed up with every answer I gave when I was being assigned a room.

I walked into a room larger than my cell to find twenty or so women (described in one of my diary excerpts). There were eight beds. How did that work? Well, I got to see first-hand how it all worked. It had to do with women who had money and were old; they were the priority. After I figured this out, there wasn't much fussing I could do, and besides, in what position did I think I was to fuss? So I settled down on the floor, and all heads turned to stare at me.

The first question I got was "Shu 2aditik?" which translates to "What's your case?" So I just said drugs, and all the women nodded as if they had known it the moment they saw me. Why? Because I was thin? Pshh. These women thought they knew it all. (Little did I know that a few months from then, I would be the one asking newcomers that question while already making my own assumptions in my head.) At least I had brought my pen, and the books that my friends had sent me when I was in my old cell; I read them all until their pages became fragile from frantically turning pages with oily fingertips. So I sat and chain-smoked, dazed and confused. *Why am I here? Where's my family? Isn't anyone going to come see me?*

Later that night, a young woman sat next to me, explaining why she was there. She had found her husband in bed with another woman, so she had tried to stab him and grazed him before he got away. She was entitled to do it; I mean, he was *cheating* on her! Right!? So, of course, knowing I was sitting next to an attempted murderer or borderline psycho, I nodded in agreement.

She then explained to me what each and every woman was doing here: what she was caught with, how she got here, who that woman was (apparently a famous drug dealer). She told me about that girl who tried to make a bomb with her own two hands, the famous runaway attempt, the girl who was pregnant over there ... I was paralyzed with fear and couldn't sleep that night. I wasn't sure if it was because I was scared of being here with these women or I was simply terrified of my situation. It was probably both, which is why I slept with my back against the wall, facing all the other women as I wrote in my diary and made coffee.

The only available facilities in the room were one Arabic bathroom and one kettle. Everything else was illegal: utensils, plates, pots, pans, anything steel or metal, any white-colored foods—rice, eggs, et cetera. All we had were cigarettes to barter with and powdered instant coffee. I wasn't upset about that, as my appetite did not come easy with the smell of us who had difficulty showering due to the lack of a shower head. We only used tubs of water, but we could heat the water, or so I thought. I didn't yet realize the electricity was available for only half the day, and our water was scarce. So my vice was cigarettes. They were all I had. The bathroom was not inviting to use with its rising odor of everything every woman in here used it for. My stomach churned every time, which did not help my IBS.

No one visited me the day after. Or the day after that. My brother and father came to me on the fourth day, telling me that they were trying to set me up to leave for another prison in Verdun, closer to home. I almost cried and begged them not to. I wasn't exactly happy where I was, but a familiar nightmare is better than a new one. They left five minutes later, leaving me with sighs and food, which I gave away.

An hour passed by, and I heard my name being called out again. I was told to pack my stuff yet again. I closed my eyes and sighed as I walked back to my room and began to pack, and right before I left the door, some women made sure to tell me I was lucky to go down there because it was "so much better." Was it? Shockingly, yes, it was, but not in the ways you might think.

Chapter Two

Lebanon, Baabda Prison,
Saturday, May 25, 2013:

This is the worst hell I've ever been in, in my entire life. I'm barely eating, and I'm barely sleeping. My left eye keeps twitching, reminding me that sleep is essential. But my brain ignores these warning signs as it keeps me awake, thinking, *What did I do to deserve this?* Nothing anyone can do is bad enough to have to live like this.

For two weeks, I kept hearing, "Tomorrow, you'll be out." I lost hope. Everyone keeps looking at me as if I'm the one who did wrong, as if what I'm saying is a lie and what *he* is saying is the truth. Nothing is more frustrating. This is all because of money and power; they are buying justice. Everyone used to ask me why I don't like Lebanon, and my answer was that it is unfair. It's unfair to allow yourself to live in a country where your opinion doesn't mean anything, what you say doesn't matter, and the truth doesn't count. Here, people think it's important to listen to what others say about us; it's our "society," they say. I've never understood this.

Why should I live a short, beautiful life according to others? What difference does it make if people say, "She married *him?*" or "Her clothes don't match." Doesn't it matter more that I'm happy with my husband or comfortable with what I'm wearing? I don't know. I don't know much anymore. All I know is I want *out* of this hellhole.

I want to go home; I want to shower, wear my clothes, and get my life back. Get my freedom back. This experience will always haunt me. I haven't cried this much in my life. I miss feeling the sun on my skin; I miss the feeling of a light wind. I miss seeing grass and trees. I miss hearing crowds of people on the street, being stuck in traffic, and hearing and seeing birds. I miss all the simple things. And that's what I want when I'm out, the simple life.

Lebanon, Baabda Prison,
Saturday, June 1, 2013:

Being in this particular prison in Baabda changed me in one minute. Now I've been here twenty-two days. I just can't stand seeing my family anymore. In my room, there are twenty, me included. There are two from Bangladesh, rude and pushy. A woman and her daughter always yell at each other and give vague answers about why they're here. There's a woman put in for the attempted murder of her husband, along with her new boyfriend, who is also in prison. She's been here for four years and had a miscarriage the first year.

A loud, obnoxious, yet caring and motherly woman has been here about a year; I'm not sure what her story is, but she's the boss of the room. Another attempted to murder her husband after finding him in bed with another woman. Three older women are the grandmas of the room, though I don't know what's up with them. One woman was put in for bouncing checks. A mother and daughter were put in for drug dealing, and there's a *huge* drug dealer who ran away from prison before and now has ten years with no chance of parole. An older woman slapped her sister a few years ago, causing her to fall down the stairs and die, and since then, the older woman has developed a split personality and now just sits here uncared for, speaking to herself.

A pregnant woman has been accused of stealing with her husband, though she says she's innocent—aren't we all? There's a woman who had her car stolen, and whoever stole it apparently fucked up a lot and blamed her for it. Ah, the justice system. Finally, another nice woman was accused of something to do with weaponry and the mafia. And one free-spirited fifty-six-year-old has almost the same story as mine—but she's been convicted for five years with no proof except for word of mouth.

Lebanon, Baabda Prison,
Sunday, June 2, 2013:

Yes, it's crazy, and in this room, shit just got real for me. I've learned a lot, but most of all, not to trust anyone, not even yourself. The thing is, I couldn't sleep last night, my first night here. I wanted to write more that I can't remember, but those memories are in my head somewhere, forever. I broke down in tears today after going to the roof, where all the prisoners go in the morning. There was barbed wire everywhere, including the roof. I ran into a crazy lesbian bitch.

I ran downstairs and spoke to a mean cop woman who informed me I did not have a court date, which upset me. Then I was told that I could not make any phone calls. And no one had sent me anything, and I didn't see anyone I knew, which was weird for me. For once, I felt completely and utterly helpless and alone.

I began to cry while walking to my room, and an old, beautiful nun stopped me. She simply put her hand on me, listened to my story, believed me, and told me to cry. She kissed my cheek and told me everything was going to be okay. It was exactly what I needed. When I came back to the room, a couple of women were pretty nice to me. It was weird but nice, I guess. I could never live like this.

Lebanon, Verdun Prison Barbar
Khazen, Thursday, June 6, 2013:

So they moved me down to Verdun Women's Prison, one more prison to add to the list. They all told me it'd be better, but it's not. I hate it. The rules here are much harsher, the guards are rude, and you can't do anything or ask for anything. I'm staying in a room with four girls. I hate this. I want to die. What the fuck is the point of getting out anymore if I'm going to be imprisoned at home? Whatever, I don't know what to say anymore. It's like it gets worse and worse and worse ...

Today is Thursday, and again, court has been rescheduled to Tuesday. I'm *so* tired of waiting. I don't care anymore. I'm *exhausted*. I've barely been writing since I got to Verdun. I think because, after thirty-something days, it just gets depressing. I've learned a lot since I got here because this place is much, *much* harsher.

Lebanon, Verdun Prison Barbar
Khazen, Saturday, June 8, 2013:

It's Saturday night. I'm going to watch our story on Al-Fasad tomorrow morning. How fucked up is that? I don't even like the boss of this place. I'm actually scared of getting out of jail and going into another jail at home. What no one gets is you learn more about life and how to live life in prison than you *ever* would outside. They'll never get that, though. No one will.

I'm so different now. I want my job back. I want to go to uni. I want to have so much work to do I barely sleep. I want to sit at home, laugh again. I want to go to the salon for my relaxing "get away from the world" moments. I want to see my friends at the infamous coffee shop or our houses. I want to eat something that I feel like eating, wear what I want, and do whatever is on my mind.

Chapter Three

Lebanon, Verdun Prison Barbar
Khazen, Friday, June 28, 2013:

Today, it's been forty-nine days. I know the Bitch is up in Roumieh. I hope they're fucking him up. Never in my life will I forgive him for trying to protect some girl he's just fucking. If I hadn't come to Verdun, I wouldn't have known any of this. I got this evidence on my own. I feel like I'm dying inside, but I'm trying to stay strong. The Bitch will never be named anything else; he named me as a drug dealer with a purse to cover for someone else, and I found out because I came to this particular prison. Isn't life funny? I wouldn't have known if I didn't come to *this* jail.

Well, I met a beautiful woman in the midst of others; however, her tattoo called out to me. I remember it clearly. "I don't want your life" is what it said. And I touched her shoulder; she turned to look at me and said, "You look so familiar!" Thus began a lifelong friendship, beginning with her knowledge of who owned the purse—the name of the girl I've been waiting to hear for months. Fate? Maybe that's what fate is: a light of love and a trusting soul who gives you everything you need and more at the moment you need it the most. You can name it what it is; it transcends words for me, as my entire body chills when I think of it.

Lebanon, Verdun Prison Barbar Khazen, Friday, June 28, 2013 *(later that night)*:

Today is the twenty-eighth. It's been forty-nine long days ... seeing everyone in prison, listening to their stories, seeing how they act and what they say. You learn things here you could never imagine seeing or learning outside. The problem is that I can't express them. I can't put my thoughts into words. Why? It's weird. I saw my mother and my sister. I missed my sister so much. My cousins and aunt wrote me letters. I miss them.

It's nighttime, and I can't sleep. The girls being tortured upstairs are screaming haunting screams. I can't. I'm done.

Lebanon, Verdun Prison Barbar Khazen, Wednesday, July 8, 2013:

Dear Diary, my father has written me two letters since I've been in Verdun—the second more pleasant than the first, if I may add. I don't know what to say to anyone anymore. Yesterday, my mom and aunt came. It was nice seeing my aunt again; she really knows what to say, and I cried a lot.

A few days ago, I had a nervous breakdown, but not like I've ever had before. I fell to the floor, my whole body was shaking, and I was completely numb. My hands were paralyzed in a position that truly frightened me. My last two fingers on each hand were folded in and couldn't be released. My teeth were chattering. It was terrible. My mind and body can't take this anymore. I'm tired all the time.

Lebanon, Verdun Prison Barbar Khazen, Tuesday, July 9, 2013:

Ramadan is tomorrow, and I thought I had so much to do before that. I thought I would definitely be out.

So, I had an investigation today … The fact that the guards from my prison who know me were with me relaxed me; odd how this prison is my "safe house," sort of, now. I just want this story to be over. I hated seeing that investigator again. Shocking how calm he was this time, hah.

Lebanon, Verdun Prison Barbar Khazen, Friday, July 19, 2013.

Time moves so slowly yet so fast. Mom also told me they've put off my case for a couple of weeks. I had a nervous break-down again. I want my life back.

Lebanon, Verdun Prison Barbar Khazen, Sunday, July 28, 2013:

Dear sister, your letters made me smile! Thanks for the great articles. I read one, and I'm starting the other; they're both great. Besides, you know me—all topics are interesting to me. The blog one was really good, and I felt a lot of it.

Ha-ha, "How's the cooking?" you ask. I'm not cooking anything because the kitchen is super appetizing! People cook for me. I miss you, and I was glad to see you those few weeks ago. It's depressing, though, how it's all behind bars. I really hate this place and don't know how much longer I can take. I'm very down all the time; my mind and body are tired. I'm tired. I have learned a lot here, and my life and attitude will be different outside. Be prepared.

I miss my classroom and my cute little students. I used to complain about being busy with work and uni and how I had to prepare lessons for my kids, then study, and have long days of running around. And in here, I'm just dead. I'd give anything in the world to have those long, hectic, busy days. Where's your "copyrighter"? Ha-ha, it's copywriter. Yeah, yeah, I'm heckling you from here. I wish I had more energy to do more things inside here, but all I do is think about everything all the time, and my thoughts are *always* jumbled up, so my brain actually hurts, you know? I miss you, and I'd love to write more and say everything, but it's gotten to a point where I don't even know what to say anymore. I love you, sis.

Lebanon, Verdun Prison Barbar
Khazen, Tuesday, August 6, 2013:

So it's Tuesday, August 6, 2013. I had a court date. It went okay, although I regret some things. They put me face to face with the Bitch, the man who first said that the purse was mine. I find only that name fitting for him, as I cannot seem to find another one without diagnosing him.

I saw all my friends. It was so nice.

Lebanon, Verdun Prison Barbar Khazen, Tuesday, August 13, 2013:

It's been three months. I'm even getting sick of the one person I can relate to here. I love her, she's a sweetheart and always takes care of me, but everybody's selfish, and I understand it. You have to be like that in a place like this.

My mom told me that she hopes I "learned a lesson." Yeah, no one will *ever* know what you can learn in a place like this unless they come here. I can't take this shit anymore; I really can't. The memory of being handcuffed in front of everyone you know and looking like shit is enough ... So I don't want to hear, "I hope you learned," anymore. Somebody save me.

Lebanon, Verdun Prison Barbar Khazen, Friday, August 16, 2013:

Yesterday, I found out a prison mate, E, was talking shit about me and spreading it through the guards as well. *I'm going to fuck her up.* I did it. I fucked her up. The "toughest girl" is scared of me now. Awesome.

Lebanon, Verdun Prison Barbar Khazen,
Wednesday, August 28, 2013:

I had a nervous breakdown again on Monday. I hate this. My
health is deteriorating. I want to leave.

Lebanon, Verdun Prison Barbar Khazen,
Saturday, October 5, 2013:

I saw a neuro doctor here in prison. She prescribed me anti-
depressants, and .75 milligrams of Lexotanil in the morning
and .75 milligrams at night. I hide them in my gums and take
a few at the same time. I'd do anything to pass the time. I
feel like I'm never going to be taken care of properly. I'm so
tired of being tired and in pain all the time. My body is tiring
out, and I can't keep going like this without being taken care
of. I have to wait till Tuesday to even do anything about it.

Lebanon, Verdun Prison Barbar
Khazen, Monday, October 21, 2013:

Family came today and gave me the "I hope you learned your
lesson" speech. I hate that speech, and I would have assumed
that people would just assume I learned my fucking lesson
after five months. I really haven't been okay lately. I'm sick
of everything, and I'm fucking tired. I'm just so fucking tired.
My eye is infected. Fuck.

Lebanon, Verdun Prison Barbar Khazen,
Wednesday, November 13, 2013:

Yeah, yeah. It's been a while. I haven't been able to write in a while—just not in the right mindset.

Lebanon, Verdun Prison Barbar Khazen,
Monday, November 18, 2013:

Yeah, it's my twenty-third birthday, and I have to admit it was the most depressing of days. So my prison roommate, Y, organized something with the whole prison to take us out to the "nozha." (The fucking nozha ... it's a small sidewalk with walls covered with depressing graffiti and, like, seven layers of fences.) They sang "Happy Birthday," and they got me cake! I'll never forget it. It made me happy for a bit to feel some love from people on such a depressing day. It was the first time the whole prison even did something like this.

Chapter Four

"I think that we're all mentally ill. Those of us outside the asylums only hide it a little better—and maybe not all that much better after all."

—Stephen King

Lebanon, Verdun Prison Barbar Khazen, Wednesday, August 28, 2013:

I had another nervous breakdown on Monday. The same feelings overcame me, where my fingers became numb, my teeth chattered, and I lost control—of everything. I hate this. I want to leave.

Lebanon, Verdun Prison Barbar Khazen,
Monday, September 2, 2013:

I was watching the end of *London* last night. There's a sentence Sid says that applies to how I feel toward everything right now: "You don't deal with it, it deals with you." Yeah, exactly. I can't believe it's already September. I hate this place. I've never felt so fucking ugly, and I just can't stand myself. I even caught lice from a beggar and felt even worse. I'm prepared to burn my head if this medicinal shampoo doesn't work. When is this nightmare going to end? I'm in hell, and I need to get out.

It's been almost four months of just living as an innocent person in jail, awaiting their fate. I keep remembering all the good times and memories I have. I can't stop myself from thinking, and it's killing me, considering I don't talk to anyone about what's in my head. I feel like I'm going crazy, and that's how I'll be seen. I have a passion burning inside of me, with a simultaneous feeling of darkness lurking for the rest of my life. I want to get out and do something, but I'm lost. I don't know how to do much anymore other than survive.

Lebanon, Verdun Prison Barbar
Khazen, Monday, October 14, 2013:

Yes, it's been a while. I went to the hospital and came back. I've been diagnosed as "severely depressed" because of nervous breakdowns and panic attacks. Yeah, no kidding. On the eleventh, I passed the five-month imprisonment mark. I feel lonelier than ever. I called my grandma today for the first time in five months … She cried so much it broke my heart. I miss her like hell.

Lebanon, Verdun Prison Barbar Khazen, Monday, October 21, 2013:

I cut off writing yesterday to talk to the nurse. I found out why my roommate is angry, and now I'm angry. She thinks I don't give her enough attention and I'm giving S, my other roommate, more attention, which is just fucking childish and annoying. I need attention too, and she barely gives it. So what now? I'm really not in the mood, though. We're in prison; we're going to play children and get angry with each other and not speak? Fine. That's just fine. I don't want to worry about this shit anymore.

My mom and dad came today. I really want Dad to come alone. They told me my court date to find out the verdict might be this week. I want to know before, though. How trippy it is waking up to yelling down the corridor, "Free Bird—court."

I'm bothered. I'm not okay. I feel like shit. I just want to finish and get the fuck out. I'm sick of people, I'm sick of the prisoners, I'm sick of the people I'm living with, I'm sick of this room, I'm sick of this prison, I'm sick of the childish attitude these prisoners have. I'm so fucking sick of it. Of all of it. It's easier not to talk to anyone and keep everything to myself. I have the song "Wait for Me" stuck in my head. I can barely remember the lyrics, but I love it.

Lebanon, Verdun Prison Barbar Khazen, Tuesday, October 22, 2013:

Me and my roommate made up, which is good. She'll always be like a sister, and sisters go through this, so it's okay. But now the other roommate is giving me attitude. I'm really not in the mood. Whatever, we'll see.

I spoke to Dad today. I'm tired. My eye is infected. Fuck. I'm so tired.

Lebanon, Verdun Prison Barbar Khazen,
Saturday, January 11, 2014:

I woke up to my favorite guard whispering in my ear, "You got bail, but don't look too excited!" That's only because while we are happy for each other when we get released, the feeling of envy and emptiness surrounds us. I couldn't believe it. I told one of my roommates, and while she was happy for me, I saw the depth of feeling within her eyes.

Four o'clock came around, and our cell doors were locked for a final shutdown, one by one. And I just waited, empty-minded, not believing I was going to leave. But the lost feeling of hope elevated. I finally heard my name. "Get up, pack, say goodbye, and you have two minutes before we shut the doors." I was rushed and disoriented, and I grabbed a few items of memorabilia and left the rest to my roommates with hugs, kisses, and tears in my eyes, wondering what kind of a world I was going into.

The drive home was silent, and my uncle surprised my entire family. I still don't know how I feel, but I know I couldn't take in the beauty of the world. Later, I researched to find out that it takes time for your eyes to readjust to a larger perception when you have been in an eight-foot-long cell room for months. While that made sense later, I walked into the house with a room full of my family and love, and I instantly felt overwhelmed.

I needed a shower. Although I used to take thirty minutes, I jumped out in two, and my sister couldn't believe it. She looked at me and asked me why I showered so quickly. I guess I didn't realize how fast I was, but that's what I was used to, a scarcity of water through a bucket shower. I was confused seeing the toilet and the flushing system; as I pressed it and heard the wonderful sound of plumbing, I smiled to myself.

Chapter Five

Lebanon, Monday, June 8, 2015:

I mean, just fuck off. Two days ago, I read a news article about my case for the millionth time. My name was mentioned, by the way, just in case anyone forgot! Isn't that supposed to be illegal? Oh right, I forgot, I'm in Lebanon ... If only this country could just be a little more open-minded, a little more educated about the ongoing life outside of this stupid shit people love calling their country. I see no reason for one to hold pride in such an unjust state. How is it okay for a fourteen-year-old to be found in a pub, drunk off his ass, and then proceed to ride a motorcycle home, either with no license or a bought one and of course with no helmet on? How? How the fuck is this okay, and is it *not* okay for someone to smoke a joint or two?

Here, I'll even give you some facts. No one in history has ever died of an overdose of marijuana. People do die from smoking cigarettes or drinking alcohol. Both are 100 percent legal in this country—at any age, may I add. I say this because I have witnessed, over and over again, children (and by *children*, I mean anyone under eighteen) buying cigarettes, drinking alcohol, and riding motorcycles while drunk and smoking a cigarette. Is that okay? Is that okay with you, the police officer who yelled at me for four and a half hours about how I smoked a joint one day and now I'm the biggest drug dealer? This is your induction?

I feel every voice deserves to be heard. I believe in democracy, and *yes*, I am proud of being an American while I surrender my Lebanese identity. "Why?" you may ask. Simple—because in my country, I am not punished for doing something legal on reasonable grounds, while here, I am detained for smoking a joint and causing no harm. Well, that's how I see it. Legally, I am being accused of dealing drugs, but I can't even say it. How unlike me.

Because of this, I had panic attacks, and now, I consume three different types of medications a day to calm me down. And still, I have no calm as I did before because of the anxiety that has been constantly instilled in me from this stupid fucking experience. It's an insane deconstruction. *Deep breath.*

I could say more, I could go on for hours, but I'm going to stop here to be polite to you. The best part is that I learned more from this experience than I would have my whole life. I'm living to the fullest I can to be the happiest I can by surrounding myself with the support I know I need. And so should you.

Lebanon, Saturday, June 27, 2015:

I don't feel like I've been really "free" at all the last couple of weeks. But when I come down to it, I can't really summarize exactly what I have been doing. I'm working to close off my debts with lower-than-minimum-wage paychecks, and I go home. I haven't even the energy to see my friends, except for one. I don't know why. I love them so much; they're the ones who stood by me through this whole ordeal when everyone else left me to rot inside, spreading all kinds of shit throughout the world. Yes, the world. Even my childhood friends, whom I haven't seen in years, have heard my story. The twisted tale is what they know.

Some people think I'm still locked up. It makes sense; I barely use my Twitter account, I barely use my Instagram account, and I've never liked Facebook, so I don't even have that. I used to be active. I used to go out, laugh, and post things all the time. But the thing is, I'm not sad about who I am right now. I'm really not. I'm content. I feel like I need to cut myself off from the world for a while with one person and just take an extended vacation away from everything. I can't believe I'm still not allowed to travel. What a country.

I have court on Tuesday. My ex has subpoenaed me. Yes. He expects me to go up there, in front of the judge and the seventy other people involved in the case, and defend him. He's quite the character, I must say. Except I'm not going to do that; I'm going to do the exact opposite. And I'm a little nervous about it, I have to admit.

I'm tired of all of this. I'm tired of telling my "friends" about when I have court or whatever because I feel like there's no connection. What's the point? Who cares? It's not like they can do anything about it. I have to deal with this on my own. Don't I? I feel like I should. I feel like this is something I need to do on my own.

Forgive the rambling. I woke up late today, and my mind is a blur right now.

Lebanon, Wednesday, July 8, 2015:

So it's been a while. There's a reason for that. Court was on Tuesday. It didn't go as well as I thought.

Lebanon, Tuesday, June 30, 2015:

I walk into the courtroom. It's filled with parents of prisoners, and soon, the prisoners walk in handcuffed and loved by their families and me. I see a few people I lived with inside and a couple of men I haven't been able to hug in twenty-six months. The judge begins, and his speech takes about an hour before we get to say anything at all.

This time, I was called by my ex, the main man in the file, to be a witness to a night that happened a week before we got caught. I realize that they are just using me as his alibi. This is idiotic on two levels: (1) I get nothing out of this but to defend the "main man" from whom I've been trying to detach myself from day one, which therefore looks terrible on my end, and (2) the alibi doesn't even make sense. I actually think his lawyer doesn't know what an alibi is. The thing is, he is being accused of giving B a load of drugs at 5:00 p.m. on the Saturday before we got caught. His alibi is "Impossible. We were all at dinner at nine. My girlfriend was there; ask her." Fine, I was there. But please, you don't have to be a lawyer (or a twelve-year-old) to question how that would acquit him of dealing at 5:00 p.m. if we were at dinner at 9:00 p.m. Just how stupid do you have to be? So I answer with "I don't recall."

I walk out, and his sister starts to run after me, yelling like a little bitch. Then his mom and dad call my whole family, asking, "How can she do this?" and "What did we ever do to her?" Really? Think hard about those questions, and just try to answer them yourselves. And here's the thing: they're my neighbors. So, I have to deal with them all the time. All the time. It's hard, it's annoying, and it's frustrating. But I have to deal with it. And the most complex part? I am told that I won't be able to travel for another six months or so.

I was so excited to move on with my life. I was excited to leave this stupid country and my fucked-up surroundings and move on. I wanted to see the world, and I wanted to discover new things; I wanted to go backpacking, and I wanted to just get on an airplane. I haven't been able to sleep properly or eat properly. I feel myself getting more and more down each day. It's hard to sleep, but once I do, it's even harder to get out of bed. I drag myself all day to finish what I have to do with minimal effort. Yeah, I admit it; I'm not the happiest I've been. I'm just happy with one thing in my life. Just one.

Lebanon, Thursday, July 9, 2015:

Isn't it funny when you suddenly look around and realize no one is standing next to you? Once upon a time, you were surrounded by all your friends.

The thing is, I feel bad. I love my friends. They stood by while I was inside. But what happened when I came out?

Everyone expects me to get over this just because I've been out for a year and a half. That's not how this works. That's not how any of this works. You cannot reduce one's experience to what you know. You cannot take this experience away from me. It's not like I'm defining myself by this experience, but this is not something to be denied. I can't help it. It is me. I will not sit and pretend like everything is okay and I'm fine. I was in prison. I slept in the same room as a killer, a murderer, a thief, and a drug dealer. Those people were my friends.

And now, I still find it difficult to move on. I cannot be hired for what I want to work for, as everyone rejected me. I can't travel; I'm stuck. I live on the same floor as the motherfuckers I have to see and deal with all the time. I will not sit down in a cafe, drink coffee, and talk about the next trip I'm going to take or the fact that "I'm so tired because I work all the time!" Well, at least you can.

Lebanon, Thursday, July 23, 2015:

I spent the rest of my days in the prison on Verdun Street. Funny, because before, I had no idea there was a prison. I thought that this ratty old building wasn't used for anything. Little did I know I'd be spending seven months and some change in that building. That building I called "home." I did. During the days I'd go to court and the two days I spent in the prison hospital, I told the guards I wanted to go back "home." I didn't mean my house; I meant the prison.

It's funny how your point of view changes so rapidly; it's difficult for me to tell you exactly when I decided that my cell would be my room. I can't say I enjoyed my time in Verdun Prison. But it was better than the rest. And when it comes down to that, yes, I did enjoy my time, and yes, I was somewhat comfortable. I hated the warden—she was a complete bitch—but I found my ways around her.

I initially moved into my room with the worst of women, lost and dazed for a while. Then I met a sweetheart inside, she asked to be moved into my room, and things just kind of looked up from there. Then S and Y moved in with us. It became our room. We turned that room into something of our own, different from all the other rooms. Maybe we did that because we were all university students, or fresh graduates, or just graduates, considering not many other women have even been to school. But the room was ours. We were pampered by Y's mom and the things she would get us from the outside. S and I became really close. I miss her so much it hurts.

We didn't have showers; we had to heat our own water in pots and shower with a bucket. That got me used to quick showers, which I can handle now. I never was able to leave the bathroom in less than thirty minutes. Now, I can shower in five if need be. We didn't have a flusher on the toilet; instead, we had to throw water there. The sound of the first time I flushed a toilet when I came out was incredible.

The place was infested with cockroaches, and the kitchen was dirty enough to turn you anorexic, which is probably why I came out fourteen kilos lighter, living on cigarettes and coffee. The food the government provided was disgusting. More so, it was poisonous.

I still have nightmares about the place, about me being dragged back in. But I don't wake up frightened. I wake up and wonder why I'm not scared of that thought. The thought doesn't scare me. Yes, I've been out for a while, but that doesn't mean I'm okay yet. That doesn't mean I can blend back into society, because I can't. I don't like society any-more. I hate this place. I hate my own home where my whole fucking family lives. And sometimes, just sometimes, I think I was happier inside. It's a sad thought, but it's not as sad as it sounds. I'm okay; I'm pleased with some things in my life right now, happy really, and not so much. But it's okay. I know I'll be fine.

Lebanon, Tuesday, July 28, 2015:

I'm longing for something—that one chance you had a long time ago to change something that would have altered your whole path. Wanting what you can't have. Needing what you do have but can't seem to appreciate while you have it till it's gone. Falling in love, giving all you have, and getting it taken away from you.

The phrase "head over heels" was originally "heels over head," and it wasn't related to love. When you were hung upside down, with your heels over your head, you felt dizzy and confused, just like love. It's hard to see something clearly when you're too involved; sometimes, you need to take a step back, and only do so if you're willing to see something you never thought was there. People tell me things, and I find it hard to be empathetic and compassionate. I don't know why; maybe my experience taught me to detach myself from those emotions because that's the only way you can survive when walking down a corridor with 120 prisoners who are all innocent. But then again, in prison, we're all innocent.

I want to travel, and I'm exhausted from this place. I have another six or so months left to go. People always say the last part is the hardest. I wonder why that is? I'm exhausted from feeling helpless most of the time. I'm exhausted from doing what I don't want to do, hearing what I don't want to hear, and seeing things I don't want to see. Yes, I'm enjoying what I have. I really am. I'm trying to embrace what I have, let go of the negative, and enjoy what I can. And I want you to do the same because when you keep in the negative, deep inside, you're losing what you have now around you. Tadeusz Borowski, a survivor of Auschwitz, wrote a book titled *This Way for the Gas, Ladies and Gentlemen*, where he mocks the whole experience in humorous sentences. And he then killed himself some four years later.

Lebanon, Thursday, October 1, 2015:

It's been a while. A little too long. I got so busy. And that's no excuse. It shouldn't be. Maybe my mind has been active a lot, and I just shut off occasionally.

So here's what's been happening. At the end of August, I got a phone call from my lawyer. He said, "You can travel now! But make sure you come back in time for your next court hearing." My flight restrictions were removed, and while still on bail, I just had to sign a paper saying I'd be right back—not that this cost nothing. The best part is that now, I can leave and travel whenever I want. What a beautiful feeling one should always feel. It's hard to see the beauty in things when you have the freedom to do so whenever you want. But when I got that phone call, it was like a weight had been lifted off me. I can finally travel whenever I want, wherever I want. And I already know where I want to go next!

Lebanon, Tuesday, October 27, 2015:

Tuesday the twenty-seventh came by, and I went to court that day. I saw all the people who hurt me, people I hate seeing in handcuffs, and people I just can't stand to look at. It was postponed. Of course, it was. What was I thinking? I went with hope once again.

Chapter Six

Dubai, Sunday, January 3, 2016:

Happy New Year's, I hope. It's been quite a while, hasn't it? Everything hurts. Even my hair hurts. Many things happened, some things I'm not allowed to even say. I debate whether I should write some of them down. I left Lebanon. It wasn't my decision. It was my family's decision. It was theirs. But it's okay, because I was the girl who put them through hell while I was in prison. I'm the girl who doesn't understand what I did to my family and their reputation, aren't I? Right, because after their fifteen-minute visitations once every three days, getting in the cars, driving back to their own homes, opening their doors to wherever, sleeping in their own beds, and simply enjoying their freedom must have been very difficult for them. See, it's not just that. Let's just say I'm the black sheep. I have my own family, the ones who have always been there for me and always been supportive. Anyway, enough about that; it's not the point. So I'm out.

The thing is, if I stayed, that'd be five years of my life just gone. I'd have to go back in. Is that fair? Seventy-two people in this stupid big case, and all of them—okay, most of them—just got five years. Why? Because why not? Half of them aren't even with evidence. The douche of a judge of our beautiful judicial system says, "I give out fives. It's my thing." And that's that. I know a lot of them. And I see a lot of them were innocent. This isn't fair. It's really not fair. And the thing is, I feel bad. I feel like I should endure it too. Is that weird?

And I do miss Lebanon. Not the idiots, not the government ... just the country. Despite all the negatives, Lebanon has a lot of positives, maybe because it's my home and where I'm from. Lebanese people and the Lebanese culture mean more to me than any other. The country itself is beautiful. There's so much to do, so much to see, so much to live. And despite what I've gone through, so many laws are being broken, and no one is looking. It's funny; it's interesting.

Lebanon is not a place where I've ever wanted to work and stay. It's not exactly the "land of opportunity." You don't see many people working up the ladder and getting far where they are; that's the sad part. But sadly, I might not see my own country for a long time. I'm not where I want to be. That's my main issue.

My biggest problem is I just signed a contract with a company for a part-time job here, but I'm on a six-month probation period, so I can leave. I want to go because this place isn't for me. So this ... this is me. I am trying to be positive and consider this a transitional period.

I'm in Dubai now, and it's different. I'm alone. I have a married sibling here; that's good. But that's about it. I live in an apartment alone. It's so empty without my sister. But I'm with my kitty. I suppose it's okay, as I might need to figure some things out, like where I want to go, what I want to do with my life. But I want to figure them out with you. Come to me. Let's do this. Let's do it together.

Dubai, Tuesday, February 9, 2016:

I don't understand. I thought lawyers were supposed to help you. Now, I'm not going to generalize, as I know a couple of lawyers practicing outside Lebanon. But the ones in Lebanon? I have seventy-two in my case; that's seventy-two lawyers I've seen, heard, and watched. And then there's my lawyer. He turned his back on me last minute, as soon as I left my country, and blurted out everything I told him in secrecy. He's *my* lawyer. He's being paid quite a lot, may I add. Did he rip off my father yet feel it was okay to do this? Why? Well, for the glory of ego: "I'm the best lawyer. I know everything." And guess what? He ruined it all for me. Everything is gone. After everything I went through, I mean, this is how he decides to end things?

From what I've seen in Lebanon, all the lawyers are dirty snakes. My close friend is still inside because it turns out her lawyer was getting paid more by her rival defendant to keep her inside. Why? Do these lawyers have zero compassion? Aren't you supposed to care about the one you're helping, the one you're taking out of prison, the one you're proving innocent? I want to file a lawsuit against the lawyers. I wish I could. I want to let out every bit of inside information I know about them, especially mine. But I'm not that low. I'm not an asshole. Well, I am kind of. But I'm not as dirty as they are. I just want the world to know. I'd like the prisoners looking for hope to know exactly who they're hiring before they're fed with lost hope.

Dubai, Wednesday, May 11, 2016:

My nightmares have been taking over me. Familiar nightmares, they don't terrify me; they're familiar. They warm my heart and turn me ice-cold as soon as I wake up. I lurched awake after having yet another of my now-all-too-familiar nightmares. They are always the same:

> *I arrive at the airport of my beloved country, where I have become a fugitive. They charged me as a runaway, as I was in Dubai when the final verdict came out. So in coming back home, I need to finish the sentencing the judge gave us. Five years. For no reason.*
>
> *As soon as I arrive, the coldness of the handcuffs hits my wrists as I'm being taken away, all while the silent surrounding is calm and collected. No one is staring; there's no shock. It's just me being taken away as everyone else continues on their governmental ride to enter their homeland. I then look around and find myself in the familiar prison where I spent my last seven months.*
>
> *A feeling of warmth washes over me. I get to see my "friends" again. I get to see the guards I love, the nurse who saved me, and the girls I eternally will think of as my family. I'm slightly aware that I'm naked of my stuff. My stuff. I need my stuff. I start to get overwhelmed, remembering that while I was comfortable here once upon a time, I'm not anymore. I begin to panic as they unlock*

*my handcuffs and sign me in. I thought they
already have my mugshot and fingerprints, so
there is no need to go through that ordeal. What
am I thinking? Is this really okay?*

*I am denied making a phone call. "Why? No one
knows I'm here! I need to tell people I'm here."
But do I really? What good would that do? It's not
like it mattered the first time.*

*I then think of a couple of people I want to see.
Just two I need to see. I keep getting denied making phone calls. Well, it's not like the first time I
was here; I was allowed to make many, if any. I
need to call them! I start to breathe heavily and
more quickly. I'm starting to panic.* I'm going to
have a panic attack *is going through my mind.*

Oh shit. I wake up, and it's cold. A rush of every memory
of the last four years just passes through me. My cat is sleeping on my head, and I realize how icy my body feels. My last
two fingers on each hand are numb. This is how my attacks
begin. Every time I have these dreams, I wake up the same
way. I tend to my bathroom needs, sit down, and love my cat
as my hands begin to get their warmth back.

Happy freedom anniversary, me.

Chapter Seven

"There's some pain that you don't share. Some pain like your fingerprints, that's all yours. All alone."

—Augustus Hill, *Oz*

Dubai, Monday, June 13, 2016:

They say home is where the heart is. That's interesting. I've been banned from my "home" since, yes, the sentence came out, and I officially have been convicted to twenty-five years as a fugitive. I think it's time I am allowed to clarify now: we were just pawns in their political game. All of us, toward the end, dwindled from seventy-two to around thirty, getting five years of jail time for drug dealing with little to no evidence. Coming from a rich and known family background, we were just used for bartering behind the political scenes. That exchanging only decreased the odds of our being released, as the lawyers and government were all making money off us. What a system.

Because I was in Dubai while the verdict was being called out, the judge decided to become angry with me, make the most of his power, and sentence me to twenty-five years—ridiculous. Everyone else agrees with me that this was only enforced in Lebanon because of corruption, as I received the exact charge a murderer would get there. I could have killed someone and gotten away with it. I won't; I just wanted to clarify how beautifully unjustified this conviction was.

My inmate buddies are awaiting their early release trial, which might happen a few months from now. With everything our case has revealed, a distribution ring in two of Lebanon's most prominent universities might not go so well. I've never met such ignorant judges, stupid detectives, and snakes of lawyers. So my options are five years unjustly in prison or twenty-five years outside. So yeah, out it is!

I'm still where I have been for six months. I am still adjusting. My job contract ends at the end of June, and I don't know what to do. I've been looking for months and months and feel like I'm underqualified for everything. I want to do this on my own. The worst thing someone can hear at a time like this is "You can't do this on your own." Why say that?

A couple of weeks ago, my laptop of five years bade me adieu. When I took it to get a check-up, I was told nothing could be done for it, and I had to say goodbye, one of the hardest things I've ever had to do. So I don't know what happened to my data. I have to save up to buy a new laptop and then check on data recovery for my old one. I cried a lot and still do now and then. All my memories, plans, and life bits are gone.

You can do this on your own. You don't have a job yet; you don't have savings because your part-time job doesn't help, and you feel like you're on a tightrope. It's okay. Live in your imagination. Live your dream. Things will happen for you. They always do, slowly. Happiness is a temporary state. Serenity is forever. Reach a state of being serene. I'm trying too—the support, the love, the comfort, the being yourself, the serenity you can have when you're in love together.

It's hard explaining "love." Someone makes you work harder to be a better you. You are constantly pushing each other and always there for each other with full support, and of course, it works better when you're physically together, but it's okay. After everything I've been through, I think I'm fortunate to say I know what love is. It's unbreakable. And that's where my home is. I can't wait to be home.

Dubai, Tuesday, November 1, 2016:

The theoretical handcuffs have come off, and my brain hurts for a while. As time moves on, the pain dissipates. I'm free now. Now what?

Broken glass is lying on the floor. The pieces are dispersed. It just slipped from my hand ... I think. Did I drop it on purpose? I can't tell. I wipe the tears from my eyes, and the tip of my finger feels so wet. Is that from me? I look down and see a trickle of blood. I don't feel the pain, and I don't understand. I do not understand much. My head is spinning, and my conscience weighs heavily on my shoulders. I'm doing it alone, and I'm okay with that. I'll be okay with that. My mind is my sanctuary, but with two contrasting characters.

Put a smile on your face, and fight your way through it. But it's so lonely at the end of the day. We all need to be dependent on something, don't we? Work, love, drugs, sex, alcohol, music, art. We live drug-infused lives.

Dubai, Sunday, April 2, 2017:

A recurring experience in jail became such a routine that when a particular time of day hit, I remembered what I wanted to forget. It was always at 1:30 p.m., and the clanging of the pots and pans against the steel doors got irritating. The guard walked leisurely with the keys jingling in her hand. "They do this on purpose, I swear to God," my roommate muttered.

Finally, the jagged sounds of the keys sliding into the hole would echo throughout the corridor. Then came the slamming and clunking of the heavier lock. Through the tiny window on this massive steel door, the women would look at the guard and tell her to hurry. They wanted their turns on the burner. The inmates scurried out into the hallway and into the small, dirty dungeon of a kitchen as soon as the guard unbolted and widened the door. Open doors in prison? That's a rarity. It's easy to forget that once you have the freedom to open a door yourself.

The guard would move on to the next door and the next until all the doors on the left side of the corridor were wide open. The women on the right side waited impatiently for thirty minutes as forty to sixty of us on one side hurriedly hovered over three working burners and an oven. We had to cook our meals and heat our water for our coffees or showers in time.

Thirty minutes would quickly pass, and we would take whatever we had done to our rooms. We unpacked our meals and water into cups and Tupperware, and the right-side inmates were off to their marathon of timed meal prep. We looked at what we had accomplished in those thirty minutes; we were pretty proud, considering this would last us until the next time we got let out, in twenty-four hours. We put the pots, pans, and anything metal or metal-like to the back of the fridge outside our rooms.

The guard walked in. "Girls, anything left around here under the restricted category?" she said while her eyes quickly dashed around the room to check.

"No," I said as she barely made eye contact, turned around, and slowly but aggressively shut our door. The keys again rattled, but this time to lock us up again—for the rest of the day. That was it; thirty minutes of being outside our room was the "fresh air" our families and visitors heard we would get to relieve them of their worries about our health.

For days, months, and years, this is what we did. Beyond the few feet from wall to wall, our eyes adjusted to a certain distance to visualize. The one time in months we went out to court, chained with our "bodyguards" of course, our minds were in unexplainable disarray. Our vision blurred, our thoughts restricted, and a negative current flowed through us, applying itself to every word said, every action done. Nothing was good. Everything and everyone was against us.

Now imagine that's how you lived your life for so long that it became the definition of life for you. And then you were let free. How would you feel?

Dubai, Friday, December 1, 2017:

Sitting on my desk on a cool Thursday afternoon in December, I was engrossed in my spreadsheet. The words *police, police station,* and *interrogation* were floating around. I felt anxious and experienced a flashback so intricately twisted I felt the rush and heat in my body. It felt so real, like I was there again. It spiraled in my head and took me back to the cold tightness of handcuffs on my wrists, arms in front, hair askew, oversized clothes, and head down in front of an outraged and vindictive judge blaring questions. But alas, I opened my eyes mere seconds later to find myself still at work with my spreadsheets open in front of me and papers strewn about my desk, only to be reminded of my reality— PTSD at its finest.

I embrace this ambiguous, almost ineffable feeling around me. It's dark but cool. The misty debris in the air radiates gray, animated with a hint of sunshine. I close my eyes so slowly I can see my upper eyelashes begin to touch my lower lashes in pure exhaustion.

Epilogue

The book flew through a small, maybe six-by-six, window high on the padlocked metal door. A small thud on the ground, and I picked it up—*Cat on a Hot Tin Roof* by Tennessee Williams. I was out of my mind at that point, but the moment I flipped the first page, I was engrossed in the Pollitt family dynamic. Mendacity—what a painful, guilt-ridden state of being.

I finished the play quickly to place it down on the filthy, grimy floor, and I immersed myself in my own state of being. I ripped out the last page and wrote till my hand ached. And to read it now—the diary of a madwoman, a free bird, whatever you want to call it—I was a cat on a hot tin roof. Oh, how it's all cooled down.

Charlotte, North Carolina,
Wednesday, January 29, 2020:

One sound took me down a path to mornings that seemed
so mundane and boring at the time. Now I think of them as
tears almost fill my eyes just enough to make my vision blur.

It's 8:50 a.m. on Wednesday, January 29, 2020. Wow.
2020. For about the twentieth time in my life, I'm taking
a practice driver's test for the third country where I am to
be licensed to drive, then run away two or four years later.
Suddenly, I look to my left and see Sylvester sitting by the
window I had widely opened that morning as I usually do.
His ears perk up, and suddenly, mine do too, out of curiosity
about what he hears. Faintly in the background, the two birds
chirp that sound like the first two *whoop-whoops* of police
sirens, if you know what I mean. I hear that sound, and all
through my body, I'm relaxed; my vision slowly starts to
blur, starting peripherally, and I remember every morning
I woke up before I had to head to CIS (City International
School Beirut) for work as a student teacher. And the flashback begins.

I would be bundled up quite nicely for the winter. With
the classy UGG boots, boyfriend jeans, tight sweatshirt, long
hair, and made-up face every day, I would get into a cab and
pay anywhere from 8 to 20 thou to get to work before 8. I
remember asking every driver, "Hey, do you smoke?" as soon
as I sat down; that was my icebreaker for eventually leading
to "Can I smoke in your car?" I always felt too guilty asking
them right away. Guilt is something I've been working on,
trying not to feel too much of it anymore.

I would get there, and as I walked toward the gate, one
hand holding a coffee and the other shoved down my purse

looking for my box of Davidoff Slims cigarettes, I could hear the faint sounds of sirens in the morning accompanied by the melodic singing of various birds. That seemed to be the same sound I would listen to every morning as I stood there, disheveled and wondering why I was up so early, waiting outside the gates of CIS anywhere between four and fifteen minutes before 8:00 a.m.—and before I had to run in and run upstairs to class to start the day as a teacher-in-training. At the click of the lighter and the sight of the flame near the tip of my cigarette, I was excited to smoke this last cigarette before going in.

I feel the ice-cold breeze on my face. The hairs on my face stand still from the cold, my eyes watching the flame and my ears listening to the chirping birds, the rustling leaves, and the light sirens in the background. I take a deep breath and inhale, exhale. My vision straightens up. It's 9:07 a.m. I snap out of it, and I look at Sylvester's beautifully piercing, predatory green eyes glare at a bird at the window, and an owl hoots; I'm back to reality.

These are the ramblings of a lost woman, a woman found years later, and a free bird caged within her mind. As the years have gone by, I have received my master's in forensic psychology, and I'm achieving my MEd in clinical psychology so I can get my license to go back home and help you.

About the Author

Ramblings from my times, experiences, and life; I want to share this with you as I continue to write and add to my life experiences while pursuing my passion in Forensic Psychology to give back to the world. Come fly with me.